BAT ODE

PHOENIX POETS

A SERIES EDITED BY ALAN SHAPIRO

Bat Ode

JEREDITH MERRIN

THE UNIVERSITY OF CHICAGO PRESS
Chicago and London

Jeredith Merrin is professor of English at The Ohio State University. She is the author of *An Enabling Humility: Marianne Moore, Elizabeth Bishop, and the Uses of Tradition* (Rutgers University Press, 1990) and of *Shift* (Phoenix Poets Series, University of Chicago Press, 1996).

The University of Chicago Press, Chicago 60637
The University of Chicago Press, Ltd., London

Printed in the United States of America

01 09 08 07 06 05 04 03 02 01 1 2 3 4 5

ISBN: 0-226-52057-9 (cloth)
ISBN: 0-226-52058-7 (paper)

Library of Congress Cataloging-in-Publication Data

Merrin, Jeredith, 1944–
Bat ode / Jeredith Merrin.
p. cm. — (Phoenix poets)
ISBN 0-226-52057-9 (cloth : acid-free paper) — (ISBN 0-226-52058-7 (pbk. : acid-free paper)
I. Title. II. Series.

PS3563.E74533 B38 2001
811'.54—dc21

00-027727

∞ The paper used in this publication meets the minimum requirements of the American National Standard for Information Sciences—Permanence of Paper for Printed Library Materials, ANSI Z39.48-1992.

for my mother, Jacquelyn Merrin

Contents

Acknowledgments

Grateful acknowledgment is made to the following publications in which these poems first appeared:

Agni: "Dear Edward Lear I Love Your Birds," vol. 44, Fall 1996
Faultline: "Southern CA"
*In*Tense*: "At the College Yesterday" (as "At the Office Yesterday"), vol. 2
Ploughshares: "Norway Maple, Cut Down," vol. 25, no. 1
Salmagundi: "Tulpenwoede"
Sewanee Review: "An American Classic," vol. 105, no. 3, Summer 1997. Copyright 1997 by author. Reprinted with the permission of the editor.
Slate™ Magazine (www.slate.com): "Bat Ode"
The Southern Review: "The Attic"; "A Downtown Diner"
Southwest Review: "Depression"
The Yale Review: "Family Reunion," vol. 86, no. 1, January 1998

I wish to thank the Ragdale Foundation for a residency during which some of these poems were completed. As always, special thanks are due to Diane Furtney for her immeasurable assistance in the work, and the life. "Day Trip" references two of her poems, "Space" and "The Only Thing."

I

Family Reunion

The divorced mother and her divorcing
daughter. The about-to-be ex-son-in-law
and the ex-husband's adopted son.
The divorcing daughter's child, who is

the step-nephew of the ex-husband's
adopted son. Everyone cordial:
the ex-husband's second wife
friendly to the first wife, warm

to the divorcing daughter's child's
great-grandmother, who was herself
long ago divorced. Everyone
grown used to the idea of divorce.

Almost everyone has separated
from the landscape of a childhood.
Collections of people in cities
are divorced from clean air and stars.

Toddlers in day care are parted
from working parents, schoolchildren
from the assumption of unbloodied
daylong safety. Old people die apart

from all they've gathered over time,
and in strange beds. Adults
grow estranged from a God
evidently divorced from History;

most are cut off from their own
histories, each of which waits
like a child left at day care.
What if you turned back for a moment

and put your arms around yours?
Yes, you might be late for work;
no, your history doesn't smell sweet
like a toddler's head. But look

at those small round wrists,
that short-legged, comical walk.
Caress your history—who else will?
Promise to come back later.

Pay attention when it asks you
simple questions: Where are we going?
Is it scary? What happened? Can
I have more now? Who is that?

Zoo Bus

A few sycamore leaves falling—
the sort of coolish,
between-seasons morning
when red cars look their best.
An honestly azure sky.
And if you take the bus
to the zoo from downtown,
admission is free. On

the hour-long ride, everyone
is looking pretty happy,
the way shoppers looked
in midsummer farm markets,
picking out tomatoes,
berries, melons, corn.

We fill our mobile room:
an older person in pink
overflowing her wheelchair;
from the halfway house
a polite, sedated group
supervised by a peppy woman
who grins and says "Hey!"
while giving high fives;

a girl-mother with a noisy,
inquisitive three-year-old boy;
a teenager, scrutinizing
the same part of the Sports Page
for over half an hour;
and myself, stealing glances
by way of the tinted glass
at the oblivious,
obstreperous child.

Debouching, our bunch
(assorted in color, class,
and level of sanity) files
through the gate and joins
the pre-arrived group
of lightly tanned mothers
pushing luxury strollers
of sunblocked toddlers
in colorful outfits with hats.

"Look at the baby giraffe, Honey!
And there's his Mommy!"
(Skinny, with huge feet,
the five-foot baby is female,
but the preschooler is a boy.)
"See the pretty kitty!"
(Meaning the snow leopard
dozing, or trying to,
in a cramped cage,
markings like paw prints
up and down its back fur.)

In these Mommy-versions, all
the animals are un-dangerous,
with strong family values.
"Look at the teddy bear!"
(But not right this second:
that toy-sized Koala
has a ten-inch erection!)

Well, we all have versions:
Me, I'm transfixed by the antics
of droll, fat prairie dogs—
sliding on brown bellies
down their short dirt hills,
popping like pinballs
in and out of holes.
I pity the striped white
Bengal—bored, twitching at
flies and loud traffic sounds.
(Why did they put him
just under the highway?)
Fine with me when he sprays
piss through the double fence
onto a small, heckling crowd.

The flamingoes hold their poses,
the toucan hops. Here comes
an Amish family around
the gorilla enclosure: four
girls in white caps and black,
apronlike dresses; two boys
in straw boaters and purple
shirts with black vests.

(They do not look at us
trying not to look at them.)

At three, the bus heads back.
Like separate species across epochs,
some passengers have persisted,
some have dropped out,
a few newcomers appear.

Here's the pink woman,
chatting with a social worker
who evidently never stops
working: "It sounds like you're
doing everything you need to
to reduce your stress levels."
Up front, a different female voice
confides loudly to the driver:
"You know where Jesus lives?
On Venus. That's right!
In the Valley of the Virgins."

Across the aisle, without
his paper and staring at nothing
—peltless, hoofless, hornless—
the teenaged boy sprawls.
Slightly sunburnt and tired,
most of us are buzzing
sociably and prenocturnally
in trios or pairs. On
the other side of the Plexiglas
the afternoon sky is still blue.

Long Distance

Lately, my daughter and I speak
by way of cats. This week,

she phoned to say she bought a female
tabby kitten, which with her huge male

Maine Coon now makes two—
like her married woman friend who owns two.

I tell her I've been feeding a stray.
Her new kitten has to stay

inside; my passing companion is not,
by the rental agreement, allowed. What

time I can, I spend
on the stoop, but mostly "my" cat and I fend

for ourselves. My daughter observes
that cats will do whatever serves

their pleasure, like her two-feline friend
who bought designer towels last weekend—

which was when my daughter's
on-and-off-again boyfriend moved in with her

again. (That last fact's not overtly in our text,
but I hear her call to him in the next

room, stage-casually.) Two
cats and a tall, faltering man. You

think I don't know what she
is telling me?

And if her kitten with its comical,
big ears and symmetrical

stripes might stand in for a baby
while she finishes her degree,

what part does "my" cat play? On the phone,
I describe this animal I don't own.

She looks like a lioness, I tell
my daughter. All

her coat is,
as her eyes

are, gold. She puts me
in mind of words like "tawny,"

"topaz," "amber";
sprawled on late summer

grass, she conjures "Kenya,"
"veldt," "savannah,"

then "impala" and other prey—
beauty impossibly far away.

There is one behavior
I don't describe to my daughter:

that she rubs her opportunistic head
against my leg after I've fed

her; then, having made sure
I'll be here for her,

that I'd like to see her every day,
stiff-legged, she steps away.

Day Trip

—for D.

The small arrangements in the car.
Want this window open a little more

or less? More heat
on your feet?

The single passenger stretches to reach
the driver's purse from the backseat,

searches, and then
hands over clip-on sunglasses just when

the light changes to red.
Now that the highway speed

is steady,
a splash of coffee, maybe,

from the thermos wedged between the sack
of food and door? (The compact

car's a stripped-down model, so
there's no CD, tape, or radio

station to negotiate, but driver
and passenger would concur:

jazz, most likely, old
and cool and loud.)

Travel that's casual
and local,

not like the singular,
compressed September

week in Amsterdam—of glinting
grachts and paintings

known for years only as prints;
of "brown bars," *frites*

met mayonnaise, and the Deco luxury
of the Tuschinski

Cinema—and where any way you look
each narrow vista's like

clicking to an excellent new
slide on a View-

Master. Now these broad fields, seen
in passing: a dozen ewes with twin

lambs, mostly black; a patch
of roadside redbuds; one flat swatch

after another of taupe, gray, brown,
every now and then

the merest flush
of green, a watercolor wash.

Next, a white poplar in a new-mown yard
("a rabbit tree," you said);

the gray verandah on that manse, where
last century's corrupt and jovial mayor

probably chugged straight
bourbon; and that,

up there—no, not a crow, a hawk!
To talk

or not talk, free
of working days' inevitably

fatiguing, forced demeanor;
free to see without being seen (or

only by each other).
We plan another

trip to Europe: autumn
after next, to Belgium

on a Bruegel hunt
(and while we're there to Ghent,

to see the Altarpiece?).
All our trips are practice

(you said once, or I did)
for disembodied,

future travel:
out the window, blue Rigel

in our Orion arm of the Milky Way. And,
moving around

through the Local
Group, M31 (opal

Andromeda), and the Pinwheel (M33)
with its bursting star nurseries.

I'd like a snack now—would you?—
while we head farther into

the Virgo Cluster. The ride
is free and comes supplied

with state-of-the-art radio.
In the mood for "Mood Indigo"?

Vision (did you notice?)
is perfect, no pain exists,

and we pass the Whirlpool
to "Satin Doll."

Turn it up! What luck!
This whole program's the Duke.

Dear Edward Lear I Love Your Birds

The Red and Yellow Macaw resplendent—
And clearly your puff-chested model,
Arching head over the arc of half-extended
Red yellow blue wing, intended us to look.

My first was in kindergarten in Oregon,
A Robin in profile and colored correctly,
But with four four-toed feet. Teacher
Pinned it on the wall, and I was
Humiliated by Open House laughter.
A child who felt, can still often feel wrong.
Hundreds of ornithological lithographs
Beautifully right, but you felt wrong.

Also I love your Salmon Crested
Cockatoo so Parisian-chic,
And your backward-S-necked elegant
But clearly low-IQ Flamingo on one
Foot. Your Toco Toucans and gold-eyed,
White-V-eyebrowed-or-seagull-eyebrowed
Spectacled Owl. All earning scientific,
Artistic respect, polite patronage,
Upper-crust meals, but little money. All
Made before the age of twenty-five.

Birds of course are phallic, though without
Apparent sexual organs, and beaks also,
Like the large noses in your Nonsense books.
Great travelers birds are as you were,
Darting everywhere and making sketches
For imitative formal landscape
Paintings for which you're not remembered,
Following your odd-shaped nose to
Rome Corsica Corfu Malta Egypt.
In Albania you were pelted, but
In Petra your pockets were rifled. In India
More seizures, in Salonika counting Kestrels.

Is it coincidental your name
Rhymes with fear fleer tear queer?
I don't think so. Bless you because
You "Never," a biographer tells us,
"Showed any capacity for flattery."
Sad single man who gladdened children,
The young Charles Pirouet for instance,
Dashing off for his amusement The Light
Green Bird The Pink Bird The Yellow
Bird and thirteen others in your hotel
In northern Italy in 1880,
Though nearly blind at sixty-eight.

Are you comfortably nested now in what
You referred to as "the next eggzi stens"?
I don't think so. But thank god when
You were dying in San Remo, rheumatic
And feeble, one servant for company,
On good days you could be moved to

The little villa's terrace. It was dim
Spring, with ten new Pigeons trying
To fly from the railing: "A great diversion."

An American Classic

A mom bakes apple pie, and a blue-eyed boy
possesses his mother almost absolutely,
repeatedly claiming her attention when

she tries to talk to his father or comes close
to kissing the stranger—a charismatic man
all three adore. The technicolor movie

is well directed: even the boy's dog,
gamely swimming a stream or sneaking with him
into the bar, turns in a better-than-average

canine performance. Twice the worshipful boy
watches the stranger fight: with his fists;
then (bespurred and white-hatted) with his gun.

The fights are staged in a makeshift town comprised
of rude plank buildings underneath blue peaks.
Everywhere is rich American mud.

The gunman is not, as such men must have been,
obnoxious and psychotic. With the father
he labors to break a tree stump from their yard

and never snaps at the boy who tags along
like some blonde dog. The parents' anniversary
falls on a rowdy, crowd-scene July Fourth.

After that, a Confederate veteran gets shot
by a gunman called in by the cattle baron,
a man dead set against farmers and the future.

The rag-tag settlers bury the Alabaman
to harmonica strains of "Dixie" and "Taps"
while the camera pans (showing life goes on)

to a nursing foal. The good gunfighter knows
to control himself, hold back for the big event,
his shootout with the hired gun, name of Wilson.

He knows, when pressed, to shoot both straight and fast
and then ride out of town, untarnished always,
a hero to the careworn, pretty mother

and her slow-witted, openhearted husband,
and to us, at home again and finding
ourselves in the practical but yearning woman,

the stolid sodbusters and hothead reb,
the bitter cattlemen whose day is done
beneath the Grand Tetons where this takes place;

ourselves in sneering Wilson, and the mud;
above all, in the boy who shouts "Come back!"
after the hero, wounded, vamoosing on his horse.

II

Tulpenwoede

("Tulipmania," or "Tulip Madness," a mass speculation in tulip bulbs in Holland during the first half of the seventeenth century, with widespread ruinous effects)

Suddenly, just one Thing,
the consummation of all craving,

for possession of which you would
(and people did) trade your world.

Gone, the family brewery; the oxen
and flour mill; every florin

put away against hard times, for old
age, the dowry of a child.

For what did you gamble?
Of what was it a symbol?

Poor neighbors grew rich on
Virgin and *Miracle*; *Paragon*

of Perfection and *General Van Eyck*.
What might your own unfurled fortune be like?

The greatest risk—
doesn't it make the best magic?

Farewell to the plodding life, yesterday's news!
Reach out and choose

one bulb, with who knows what defects—
a cold fist, food for insects

and moles. But here is the charm:
this same Dutch soil that harms

most other plants makes this one grow
fantastical and rare—no

longer smooth-edged but exotic,
ruffled; not one hue but hectic

as a New World parrot. Forms unfold
from diseased ground, worth a king's gold.

So you'd heard, so you dreamed. And the more
you invested, the more

it had to be true.
When the market failed, who

could believe it? How many raved on,
even bankrupt, in prison?

A strange madness
—picturesque but not harmless—

in the seventeenth century,
and in Holland only.

Nothing like what we in our own
lives have heard of, or known.

Depression

He does nothing—
having great trouble moving,

being so heavy. A has-been
fatted on grievance, an old actor gone

on drugs. His color, no color:
an overcast sky; the dolor

of a pebble lifted from the stream
where it once seemed

bright-hued, holding promise,
a pretty egg. He is

without affection or affect.
Over the eye, a cataract.

He does not become expansive
like joy or true grief, which have

their social rituals that shed
a sort of light. Instead,

a space-time funnel
or hole: a mere spoonful

of dense stuff,
the undoing of stars. Enough

has been said of his
appetite for ashes.

He has no clear
shape—a heap of laundry, a smear

of dead bug. Glimpsed piecemeal
in a pile

of long overdue books, last
night's greasy dishes; in low test

scores, a pimple, a bruise.
He smothers good news

the way eight-hundred-
pound sea lions, absentminded,

will squash their own young.
Think of *carcass*, *failure*, *dung*,

paralysis, *bad breath*,
envy. In his house, no hearth-

fire or music; spiders there
suck hopes dry.—You can stare

at the floor or repeat, "No, no."
But where I have been, you will go.

Film Noir

Leaves clatter
in the hot September

breeze—a day like summer,
but the season's over.

Walking,
then slowly sipping

coffee, then
walking again,

all afternoon
a kind of itch between

my right index and middle
fingers: I want to fiddle

with something—a cigarette or
pen, I'm not sure

which. I imagine
the satisfaction

first of one and then
the other. The pen

would mean,
of course, ambition

for everything, fame
(the marquee name

in lights appeals);
but just to feel

again in motion
that still-operative old machine,

myself,
could be enough.

To hold, on the other
hand, first one and then another

cigarette would mean giving
up: something like reading

yet another mystery, isn't it,
except that you're complicit

in the murder? Down
the cafe's beige and brown

Formica counter, a younger
woman smokes, reading the paper.

Long ago, I gave up
that form of giving up,

but her Salems in their green
softpack look good. I've been

so goddam good so long
I long

to be bad: lawless, offhandedly
cruel, free

of the crush
of common sense—farouche

in satin, like
some white-skinned, black-

lipped actress on
a huge, indifferent screen.

Barbara Stanwyck,
in *Double Indemnity*. A quick

flash—the taciturn salesman's
proffered match: fans

glimpse her bleached blonde
hair against the shadows and

the exchange of gone-wrong
glances. The long

drag. *Take it all in,*
baby (Why not?); *and then*

(He aims, we know
by now what's coming) *let it go*.

Impediments

Those we construct, and those put in our paths:
poverty, disability, a history

of disfigured or absented parental love,
recurrent fatigue, the clutter of distraction,

manifold forms of fear and self-abuse.
The blue world's beautiful vastnesses, yet who

on it moves freely? On the late-night screen,
each element completed in each skater's

clocked routine seems to defy, undo
for everyone one more entrammelment.

The *flying camel* (say, chronic depression?),
triple lutz (agoraphobia),

double axel (alcohol addiction),
spiral (job loss), *double salchow* (divorce),

triple flip/double toe loop (major surgery).
And look! A *quadruple/triple combination*!

No obstacle in sight on the White Ring.

Hotel Breakfast with an Old Classmate

Pale and too thin, eating barely
enough bland food to stay alive,
while envy of nearly everything gnaws
on you—adding salt, guzzling
wine, picking his gross teeth—
old college classmate, not quite a friend,
is this how you must spend
the middle of your life?

This morning in the outside world
that does not seem to interest you,
red leaves gust in a cool wind,
clear drops depend from the wires;
children in yellow slickers ride
yellow buses. Which will life favor?
Aren't we all told to savor
time passing, since time passes?

You tell your beads of miseries,
thinking I have all the luck,
and, never asking, never know
whether I ache for my love or child,
whether I savor the days going by,

or how envy has eaten at me
—sloppily, with his dripping grin—
about our much more famous friend,
whom envy also, for the great dead, eats.

Southern CA

Where a slight rain is forecast as
serious "weather," movies make the six o'clock news;
brown pelicans fish the wave breaks,
orange trees fruit in January, and everywhere
are Asian faces, Hispanic
ones, bougainvillea on stucco walls, Spanish-tiled roofs;

health clubs, vintage cars, upscale malls,
low-slung peach-teal-avocado condos on hillsides,
wharves, poppies, bird of paradise,
lungo, macchiato, espresso, cappuccino,
tall palms, squat palms, skateboards, wetsuits,
hawks, plovers, red-beaked gulls, and the Western Sandpiper—

a wind-up bird, all legs and beak,
racing oceanward over water-glazed sand, tipping
like the adze-head oil rigs close to
shore, probing (like a robin on sodden lawn?), zipping
back landward, fractions of an inch
ahead of the surf, and not once submerging its feet.

Ugetsu

—Ugetsu Monogatari *(1953), directed by Kenji Mizoguchi, based on stories set in sixteenth-century feudal Japan*

"I am not a ghost," croaks the dying man,
lying in his wooden boat that has drifted
up to the other small boat on the lake,
full of the main characters in the mist.

But the Lady in her phantom mansion is.

In front of her father's empty, moaning armor
she dances stiffly, seducing the guileless potter
who left behind the wife he'd dreamed of robing
in noblewoman's silks. Hatched in the midst
of chaotic feudal warfare, his half-baked plan:
time to head out and make a killing on pots.

They have a small son, silent as a corpse
slung on his mother's back, except for shrieks
when she is robbed of rice cakes tucked in her bosom
and speared for no reason by a starving soldier.

Also through the membrane, mother to spectre.

Dead or alive, the women are all sad:
The potter's wife, and the other peasant woman—
raped by soldiers and become a whore

after her foolish husband abandoned her
to play at hero in a samurai suit;
and the Lady, slaughtered when her father
was overpowered by another Lord,
so "she never tasted the pleasures of love,"
mourns her loyal, melancholy nurse.

The men, who all want stature in women's eyes,
only make more ghosts in a ghostly world.

When at the end the widowed potter returns
and pats the head of his silent, living son,
it hardly makes sense. Why is the boy still living?
And who can be sure of what is phantom or real,
since anyone's hopeful life is a boat in fog?

But for a time, the world of rape and plunder
is still: chastened, he listens to the voice
of his ghost-wife—"You have become my ideal
man, but now I am in another world"—
and sits in the hut at his wheel and builds a pot.

From a Summer Porch

—Lake Forest, Illinois

One small, white-wicker
rocker in the corner;

an unpainted, wicker side table,
damaged, with a wobble;

a seven-dwarves-size
bed; one old chaise

longue; and this blue-green,
sun-blistered desk, facing the greens

of maple, ash, and lawn.
Late morning, and since dawn

I've sat here, by turns thinking
or not thinking.

It feels as if I were born
to sit in one

place thinking
or not thinking—

woolly-minded and foolish,
sometimes, as a sheep! I wish

that I were wise.
But as it is . . .

*

Cicadas buzz,
a crow caws;

at noon
the whole lawn

is in shadow,
there are that many trees. Below

the weeping willow
is a fountain, like another willow.

How strange life
here feels, without pressing grief

or fury
or avidity.

A blue-eyed sheep's head
drifts by. Dispersing, the cloud

transmogrifies—
a skull with gaping eyes;

then wisps regroup to make
a long-necked bird by Braque,

a trapezoidal wing . . .
I doze on the chaise longue.

*

The sky now is “darkling,”
the birds settling

down. End-of-the-day mysterious
messages in various

avian voices: a liquid trilling,
a rusty porchswing,

a third like scissors
snipping. Under

the trees, where we
live, excitedly

some distant dogs are barking. Someone calls
children home. A lull;

a mosquito intermittently
whines, making me

anxious, bites my leg,
goes off to lay her eggs.

*

Branches in silhouette
form webs or nets;

one tree makes ostrich
plumes. Pretty soon it's pitch

dark, as though the sky
were taken over by

black trees. This obliteration
of distinction—

does it almost terrify
or reassure, and why?

Oblivion
is one main

desire, but vigilance is another:
and who can ever

finally choose between
the two? And when

even this pampered gaze
and rare vacation ease

cannot quite satisfy,
not perfectly, what should I

do, or be—bathed in warmth
and rocking back and forth

(I'm in the rocker),
one night in summer?

III

Bat Ode

Downtown Columbus, Ohio, rush hour

Dead, of course, but with soft,
egg-sized black body and
scalloped, coal-satin wings—
so pretty, it was hard

not to be happy to
have the rare city sight
of it. Hyper-real
(the way death always is),

and mildly exotic;
a sidewalk frisson, break-
ing middle-aged boredom.
(Everyone, everyone

becomes predictable—
especially the young
rebels, so timidly
indistinguishable,

and the "mature" beige ones:
alike in their terror
of appearing foolish
at all costs, at great cost,

inestimable cost.)
The bat was new, intact.
Heart flutter suddenly
stopped, dropped to the pavement.

O Delicately Veined,
Neat Eared, Night Wandering.
Neither epiphanic
lark, nightingale, nor rook.

Downtown Diner

Scuzzy Michael's Diner. Briefcase
and French loaf in tow, on my way to the office,

in need of the restroom and coffee.
Inside, flashback to San Jose and my greasy-

spoon, Welfare mornings in tattered
—not purposefully or artfully tattered—

jeans; the two-egg-and-hashbrown special
I ate then, with no one from that other, well-

dressed world to breeze in and deliver
a fresh sense of failure to us hunched-over

eaters. In Michael's, a woman looked up when
I walked in, then quickly down again.

And I may have spoiled her leisurely
breakfast—probably

the chief expense and pleasure of her day.
Fifteen years ago, in San Jose,

chic department stores could terrify:
the coolly assessing, arched eye-

brows of smartly dressed saleswomen
and consumers—who could bear them?

Even if you spend more of
the little you have,

it hurts less to shop at "cut-rate,"
unreproachful stores. Long-term poverty humiliates

like childhood: you might be judged wanting,
be laughed at any moment for something

not in your power to avoid. Only,
you can't outwait it like childhood. Maybe

that woman dipping toast into egg yolk had
less passion or ambition than I had;

maybe more. She should not have been
disturbed in that small consolation

of egg. Who possesses the wherewithal
for labor or love without small

consolations? Who can live?

At the College Yesterday

This crazy colleague on the elevator
and her bright, repeated answer,

"Fine!" when no one had ventured the casual
"How are you?" Her brittle

smile. And others among us, pretending
every day not to be hurting

or frightened. Switch on
the fluorescent lights, get on

with the paperwork,
the small talk;

haven't you heard it said:
"It's better to be distracted"?

With that policy,
though, you risk insanity.

So tell me, where is it,
your soul of the moment?

Just now, mine fed
on dust under the bed,

sulking at chance,
louring in grievance.

It's 5:15 a.m., a Saturday
in late May,

and what is meant
by that insistent

robin? Did the eggs hatch? Are
the hatchlings hungry, or

being called out for
their first, fear-

ful flutter on the wire? What
I mean is, that

elevator was a terrible
place. Better a feeble

soul, exposed on a wire.
Better anywhere

than a box between floors
with sliding doors,

crushed in with strangers
and obliged to reassure

each of them. “Fine,”
you grin, “fine,” “fine.”

Memo

What about highway driving and the alteration of landscape
as you turn off to enter the ugly, inevitable
fast-food strip of another town and

suddenly wake up to how strange this cable- and wire-
bedizened American picture is? Whose idea was it,
anyway, to arrange things this way?

Or the office with recessed fluorescent lighting
and pressed-board cubicle dividers: who said
this is how human beings do their work?

When young, not the dimmest notion how a life might be
constructed, but furious determination never
to repeat things *their* way.

In the middle of my life I am in the middle of
a committee meeting. Millions-of-years-old
sea turtle species are dying

in the Gulf of Mexico from ingesting plastic rings
manufactured for six-packs of soft drinks.
Small children get slapped on buses

by frustrated, indigent mothers who control nothing
but flinching, hardening children and no one,
for fear of making it worse, can say Stop!

In the meeting we take up whether a particular
form should be filed in Winter or Spring—
a minor adjustment of local use,

the kind of regulation one well-meaning committee
assigns to another as we near the year
2000. How did we get

here—no longer vagabond in bright hues,
obsessed with rebellion and the cure
of eros—now in charge

of minute tasks within a universe vaster than our
parents imagined, and telling ourselves,
as they did, "We're doing our best"?

New Apartment

Columbus, Ohio

Homemade, slightly cockeyed,
painted a licorice green:
at the antique mall I found
(cheap, amazingly dirty)
the ideal kitchen cupboard.

Every day more projects.
Selecting and aligning:
the Deco clock just so,
the morris chair angled more.
See how the De Hooch print

echoes the courtyard view
framed by our kitchen window?
That last was D's genius stroke.
What drives us to perfect
these patched and rented rooms,

straining our modest means?
It can't be to impress;
we seldom entertain,
and, anyway, who'd praise
such unorthodox designs,

not "plain as the rose in your vase"?
Everywhere, though, arrangers
are moving and setting up
"home" as it should have been,
since it should have been perfect.

One house needs a vinyl
sofa and player piano;
another, a fantail fire screen
or plastic lawn flamingo.
Only some things are magic

enough to reclaim a part
of some particular past:
ivy arched over a doorway,
a turn-of-the-century rocker,
our frank-faced forties clock.

In the abode-as-city-state,
absolute rule offsets
a sense of powerlessness?
Or the new place is a body,
improved instead of worn

by knowledge over time?
We go on rearranging
until we're half convinced
old burdens have been banished—
ritual objects placed.

The Attic

Wherever you are is it, is in the middle
of what you're supposed to pay attention to.
For me, for instance, right now, this attic room
filled with things that happened to land together—
rolled rugs, scuffed suitcases, a wooden stool,
a pretty, carved French chair in disrepair,
and cardboard boxes stacked along one wall,
labeled in red: Sewing, Taxes, Blankets,
Extra Cookware, Winter Gloves & Scarves.
This cluttered, ruder outpost of the house
is arbitrary, but in its way arranged,
the way we like to think our lives arranged
by a higher force or being. As aging Ovid,
exiled from Rome to brute, unlettered Tomis,
writing *Tristia* and *Epistulae*,
enduring mud and cold, chose to believe
his misery had been decreed by gods:
"Otherwise," he wrote, "we are all at risk . . .
each moment a free fall into a moral void."

Meanwhile, here I am in my life's jumble.
Above the table, where Ovid in English lies,
a gilt-framed print we couldn't use downstairs

hangs on a nail that was already here.
Smaller than a standard sheet of paper,
it's John the Baptist in a fifteenth-century
green and pleasant "desert"; to his right,
a seated lamb with daintily posed hooves.
It's a toylike creature crowded in with others
(some too-large birds as well as fat, tan rabbits;
miniature does and grazing stag)—
except the lamb, of course, is *Agnus Dei*,
with thin ray lines surrounding its white head,
pink-nosed, triangular. John is resting
his cheek on his right hand (improbable,
the angle of that arm): his face is sad.
On bony ankles, his long and long-toed feet
curl inward, as if comforting each other.

I would have loved that picture in my childhood
when I sat barefoot, often solitary,
as I still do, and daydreamed over books,
as I do still, and still believed in God.
Below John in his wilderness are books.
A Beginner's Guide to Guns and *Daffodils*
For American Gardens stand side by side
with a faded paperback: *Delusion and Dream*.
Art substitutes, says Freud, for childhood play;
audience and maker both indulge
in daydreaming without reproach or shame.
"Happy people do not make fantasies."
Of course, that points to what Freud also knew:
no one is happy, we all fantasize
because all wishes can't be satisfied;
no one can even imagine a life like that.

Whatever it is you see from where you are
is what you're meant to consider. That's as far
as I go, anyway, with "decrees of gods."
These things are in the attic. In my mind,
a patchwork of facts, pleasure mixed with sadness;
a need, like everyone's, for pattern, order.
Ovid in Tomis felt it more than most.
Where "the wolves creep close and vultures circle,"
he yearned for pardon or some base, at least,
his wife might safely visit; any place
where Latin could be heard and understood.
Holding on to "Roman strength and calm,"
or trying to, amidst Scythian lice and jabber
(whether an influential reader was moved
to plead his case with great, unheeding Caesar,
or whether Caesar might grant one trip home),
he was in the middle, not in exile, really:
"It's not a mere conceit: out here, *I* am Rome."

Sweeping

Late August, sweeping from the patio
Norway maple seeds: green handlebar mustaches,
fit for elves of the last century.
If I live much longer, they'll be able to say that I
belong to the last century. The broken
half-samaras are like wings of Fra Angelico angels—
chartreuse and moss green, with touches of rust.
It makes a sort of haiku:

In the courtyard
a woman of fifty works,
sweeping maple seeds.

Mornings, I feed the squirrels,
coaxing them closer. Bits of bagel or toast;
sunflower seeds; now and then, peanuts.
Sturdy creatures with four-toed front paws
and large, round eyes. They'd do fine without me
on backyard insects, neighborhood garbage,
and occasional nestling birds—not to mention
all those maple seeds.

A woman of fifty
scatters bread
for fat squirrels.

Not exactly outdoors or indoors, neither young
nor very old. Barefoot, without makeup.
Birds visit for crumbs: two cardinals;
starlings, sparrows, house finches;
the occasional clever jay.

Whoo-oosh! goes the broom:
orange tomcat chased off
by a woman of fifty.

Norway Maple, Cut Down

November 1997

Its bare branches the winter before
were exuberant scrawls
against a blank sky about
to snow and then snowing,
or runes punctuated
by the brownish-gray
question marks of squirrels.
And this fall, the leaves
were so gold they looked heavy
as Cleopatra's burnished throne
or as some feeling unexpressed.
The one tree in the yard,
casting lace on the concrete stoop,
blocking an alleyway from view.

Our garrulous German landlady,
a Transylvanian post-War
emigrée, with no explanation or
warning ordered the forty-foot,
healthy tree cut down.
Inhabiting a squat, brick house
behind oversized security lights,
two doors from our half-double
on a pretty, Victorian street,

she'd worked years and years
in department stores, putting away
nickels and dollars for property—
more money, more property.

One more incidence of
a small or large brutality
and there's nothing you can do:
the salacious welfare worker
in charge of your case;
the ash blonde in expensive shoes
who enjoys spoiling another
woman's self-esteem with a sneer;
any of the perennial
bullies of history, who
always could line up your family
and shoot them in a ditch.

Why didn't she relent,
when on that morning—the man
waiting, tethered up in the tree—
we pleaded with her, offering
to pay the workman's fee,
and surprising ourselves with tears?
Was she trying to please (or in a way
to *be*) her father, long dead,
a farmer in the Old Country she
talked and talked about, and who had
once, she said, cut down an entire
orchard of apricot trees?

Was she prodded by a kind of envy?
Married and divorced young,

she'd never remarried;
and one time, inspecting
the apartment we'd furnished
—my partner and I, living openly
together—she startled us,
blurting, "*I* could live with a woman.
But I have bad luck. Probably,
she not work hard, like me."
Busy, self-assigned patroller
of the street—had age made her
terrified of the free-falling leaves
she complained about:
"a mess! a big mess!"?

Determined, she stood mid-yard:
white-haired, blue-eyed, seventy-eight
and stocky, in her thrift-shop
motley of flowers and stripes.
Among the bagged and unbagged
leaves that I'd just raked,
she shouted, "This is not your
property, this is *my* property.
You want a tree, move out!
Move to a farm if you want
trees!" Then, "Do it!"
to the dangling man, awaiting
his order; "I pay you. Just do it!"
It took hours, it took all day.

Leaning back in a patio chair
June afternoons, you could see
three or four layered greens
juxtaposed with blue puzzle pieces

carved by the five-lobed shapes.
Indoors, every season,
on the bone-white walls
that renters live with,
patterns of light and shade
altered as the tree altered,
like slightly rearranged
but lifelong compulsions,
and like the always available
possibility of changing your mind.